Easy Learning

Design Patterns

Python 3

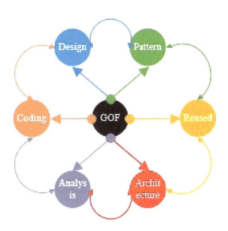

YANG HU

Simple is the beginning of wisdom. From the essence of practice, this book to briefly explain the concept and vividly cultivate programming interest, you will learn it easy and fast.

http://en.verejava.com

ISBN: 9781098531027

CONTENTS

Strategy Pattern Principle

Strategy Pattern:
Encapsulates an algorithm inside a class. Define a family of algorithms, encapsulate each one, and make them interchangeable.Strategy lets the algorithm vary independently from clients that use it.

1. Calculate Strategy Addition, subtraction, multiplication, division

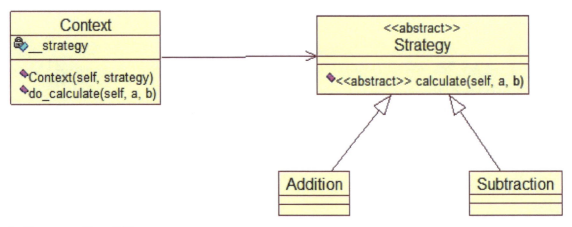

2. Create a Test File : test_strategy.py

```python
############### Strategy #################

class Strategy:
    def calculate(self, a, b):
        pass

############### Addition #################

class Addition(Strategy):
    def calculate(self, a, b):
        return a + b;

############### Substraction #################

class Subtraction(Strategy):
    def calculate(self, a, b):
        return a - b;
```

```
############### Context ################

class Context:
    __strategy = None

    def __init__(self, strategy):
        self.__strategy = strategy

    def do_calculate(self, a, b):
        return self.__strategy.calculate(a, b)

############### test ################

ctx = Context(Addition())
result=ctx.do_calculate(4, 2)
print("Addition : ", result)

ctx = Context(Subtraction())
result=ctx.do_calculate(4, 2)
print("Subtraction : ", result)
```

Result:

Addition : 6
Subtraction : 2

Strategy Pattern Case

1. Case: E-commerce chooses different banks to pay different strategies.

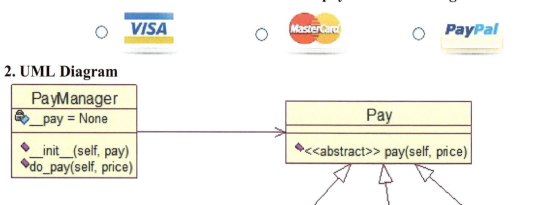

2. UML Diagram

2. Creae a Test File : test_pay.py

```python
############### Pay ################

class Pay:
    def pay(self, price):
        pass


############### MasterCard ################

class MasterCard(Pay):
    def pay(self, price):
        print("Pay ", price, " $ by MasterCard")


############### Visa ################

class VisaCard(Pay):
    def pay(self, price):
        print("Pay ", price, " $ by VisaCard")
```

```
############### Paypal ################

class Paypal(Pay):
    def pay(self, price):
        print("Pay ", price, " $ by Paypal")


############### PayManager #################

class PayManager:
    __pay = None

    def __init__(self, pay):
        self.__pay = pay

    def do_pay(self, price):
        self.__pay.pay(price)


############### test #################

print("You need to pay $25  for mobile phone ")
code = int(input("Please select payment method 1: MasterCard 2: VisaCard 3: Paypal \n"))

payManager = None
if (code == 1):
    payManager = PayManager(MasterCard())
elif (code == 2):
    payManager = PayManager(VisaCard())
elif (code == 3):
    payManager = PayManager(Paypal())

payManager.do_pay(25)
```

Result:

You need to pay $25 for mobile phone
Please select payment method 1: MasterCard 2: VisaCard 3: Paypal
2
Pay 25 $ by VisaCard

Composition Pattern Principle

Composition Pattern:

A tree structure of simple and composite objects. Compose objects into tree structures to represent part-whole hierarchies. Composite lets clients treat individual objects and compositions of objects uniformly.

1. National city tree diagram

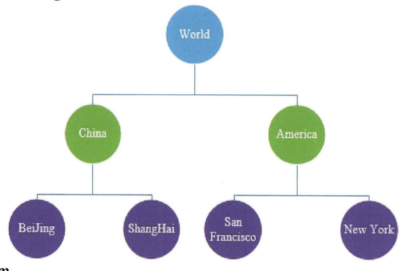

2. UML diagram

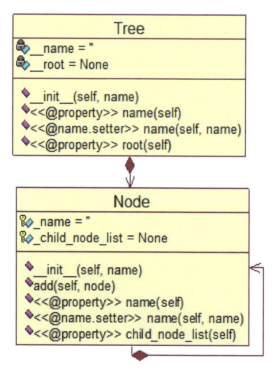

3. Create a Test File : test_tree.py

```python
############### Node #################

class Node:
    _name = ''
    _child_node_list = None

    def __init__(self, name):
        self._name = name
        self._child_node_list = []

    def add(self, node):
        self._child_node_list.append(node)

    @property
    def name(self):
        return self._name

    @name.setter
    def name(self, name):
        self._name = name

    @property
    def child_node_list(self):
        return self._child_node_list

############### Tree #################

class Tree:
    __root = None # root node
    __name = ''

    def __init__(self, name):
        self.__root = Node(name)

    @property
    def root(self):
        return self.__root

    @root.setter
    def root(self, root):
        self.__root = root
```

```python
    @property
    def name(self):
        return self.__name

    @name.setter
    def name(self, name):
        self.__name = name


############### test ##################

tree = Tree("World")
root = tree.root

china = Node("China")
root.add(china)

beijing = Node("Bei Jing")
shanghai = Node("Shang Hai")
china.add(beijing)
china.add(shanghai)

america = Node("America")
root.add(america)

sanfancisco = Node("San Fancisco")
newyork = Node("New York")
america.add(sanfancisco)
america.add(newyork)

print(root.name)
child_node_list = root.child_node_list
for node in child_node_list:
    print("----", node.name)
    child_node_list2 = node.child_node_list
    for node2 in child_node_list2:
        print("--------", node2.name)
```

Result:

```
World
---- China
-------- Bei Jing
-------- Shang Hai
---- America
-------- San Fancisco
-------- New York
```

Composition Pattern Case

1. Recursively print all directories and files.

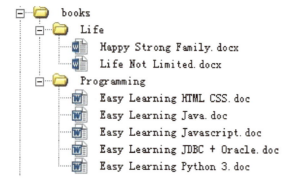

2. UML diagram

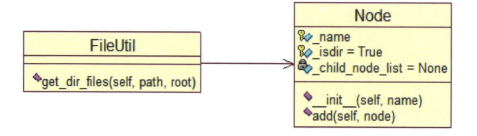

3. Create a Test File : test_file.py

Recursively print all directories and files.

```python
import os

############### Node #################

class Node:

    _name = ''
    _isdir = True
    _child_node_list = None

    def __init__(self, name):
        self._name = name
        self._child_node_list = []

    def add(self, node):
        self._child_node_list.append(node)

    @property
    def name(self):
        return self._name

    @name.setter
    def name(self, name):
        self._name = name

    @property
    def isdir(self):
        return self._isdir

    @isdir.setter
    def isdir(self, isdir):
        self._isdir = isdir

    @property
    def child_node_list(self):
        return self._child_node_list
```

```python
############### FileUtil ################
class FileUtil:

    def get_dir_files(self, path, root):
        # Get all the files in the current directory
        fills_list = os.listdir(path)

        for file_name in fills_list:
            # Determine if it is a path
            file_abs_path = os.path.join(path, file_name)
            if os.path.isdir(file_abs_path):
                current_node = Node(file_name)
                current_node.isdir = True
                root.add(current_node)
                # Recursively get_dir_files
                self.get_dir_files(file_abs_path, current_node)
            else:
                current_node = Node(file_name)
                current_node.isdir = False
                root.add(current_node)

        return  root


############### test ################
def show_all_dir_files(current_node, level = ''):
    child_node_list = current_node.child_node_list
    level += "----"
    for node in child_node_list:
        if node.isdir == True:
            print(level, node.name)
            show_all_dir_files(node, level)
        else:
            print(level, node.name)


user_dir = r"E:\books"
root = Node("books")
file_util = FileUtil()
root = file_util.get_dir_files(user_dir, root)

print(root.name)
show_all_dir_files(root)
```

Result:

books
---- Life
-------- Happy Strong Family.docx
-------- Life Not Limited.docx
---- Programming
-------- Easy Learning HTML CSS.doc
-------- Easy Learning Java.doc
-------- Easy Learning Javascript.doc
-------- Easy Learning JDBC + Oracle.doc
-------- Easy Learning Python 3.doc

Singleton Pattern Principle

Singleton Pattern: A class of which only a single instance can exist. Ensure a class only has one instance, and provide a global point of access to it.

1. UML Diagram

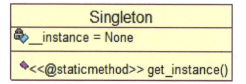

2. Create a Test File : test_singleton.py

```python
class Singleton:
    __instance = None

    @staticmethod
    def get_instance():
        if Singleton.__instance == None:
            Singleton.__instance = Singleton() # there is only one instance
        return Singleton.__instance

s1 = Singleton.get_instance()
s2 = Singleton.get_instance()

#two instances, refer to the same address
print(s1)
print(s2)
```

Result:

```
<singleton.Singleton object at 0x0000000002592240>
<singleton.Singleton object at 0x0000000002592240>
```

Template Pattern Principle

Template Pattern: Defer the exact steps of an algorithm to a subclass. Define the skeleton of an algorithm in an operation, deferring some steps to subclasses. Template Method lets subclasses redefine certain steps of an algorithm without changing the algorithm's structure.

1. **The parent class prints A4 paper, and the subclass can also set the color.**

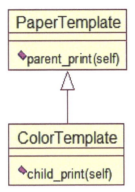

2. **Create a Test File : test_template.py**

```
############### PaperTemplate ################
class PaperTemplate:
    def parent_print(self):
        print("Print A4 Paper")


############### ColorTemplate ################
class ColorTemplate(PaperTemplate):
    def child_print(self):
        self.parent_print()
        print("Set the color of A4 paper red")


############### test ################
template = ColorTemplate()
template.child_print()
```

Result:
Print A4 Paper
Set the color of A4 paper red

Template Pattern Case

Airplane games:
Different airplane with the same characteristics, but behaves differently

1. UML Diagram

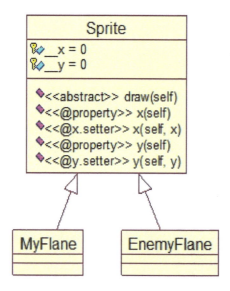

2. Create a Test File : test_sprite.py

```python
############### Sprite ################

class Sprite :
    __x = 0 # Airplane x coordinates
    __y = 0 # Airplane y coordinates

    # Draw the plane on the screen
    def draw(self):
        pass

    @property
    def x(self):
        return self.__x

    @x.setter
    def x(self, x):
        self.__x = x

    @property
    def y(self):
        return self.__y

    @y.setter
    def y(self, y):
        self.__y = y

############### MyFlane ################

class MyFlane(Spritc):

    def draw(self):
        print("My plane from the bottom of screen : x=" , self.x, ",y=", self.y)

############### EnemyFlane ################

class EnemyFlane(Sprite):

    def draw(self):
        print("Enemy plane from the top of screen : x=" , self.x, ",y=", self.y)
```

```
############### test #################

mySprite = MyFlane()
mySprite.x = 100
mySprite.y = 300
mySprite.draw()

enemySprite = EnemyFlane()
enemySprite.x = 0
enemySprite.y = 300
enemySprite.draw()
```

Result:

My plane from the bottom of screen : x= 100 ,y= 300
Enemy plane from the top of screen : x= 0 ,y= 300

Factory Pattern Principle

Factory Pattern: Creates an instance of several derived classes. Define an interface for creating an object, but let subclasses decide which class to instantiate. Factory Method lets a class defer instantiation to subclasses.

1. **Products can be created by the factory**

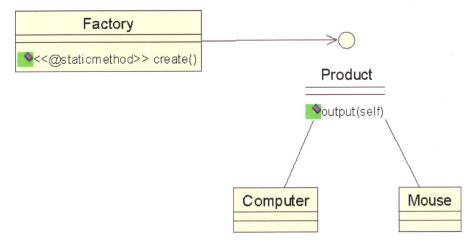

2. **Create a Test File : test_factory.py**

```python
############### Product #################

class Product:

    def output(self):
        pass

############### Computer #################

class Computer(Product):

    def output(self):
        print("Dell Computer")
```

```
############### Mouse ################

class Mouse(Product):

    def output(self):
        print("IBM Mouse")

############### Factory ################

class Factory:

    @staticmethod
    def create(type):
        p = None
        if (type == 0):
            p = Computer()
        elif (type == 1):
            p = Mouse()

        return p

############### test ################

p = Factory.create(0)
p.output()

p = Factory.create(1)
p.output()
```

Result:

Dell Computer
IBM Mouse

Factory Pattern Case

Airplane game:

Create different airplane by Factory and then shoot different bullets

1. UML Diagram

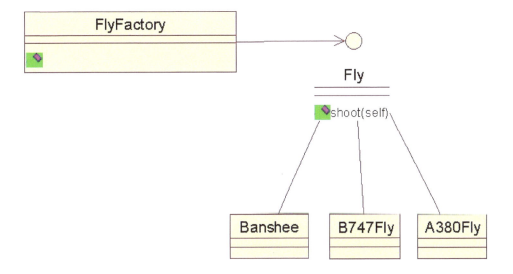

2. Create a Test File : test_factory.py

```python
############### Fly ################

class Fly:

    def shoot(self): # firing bullets
        pass

############### Banshee ################

class Banshee(Fly):

    def shoot(self):
        print("Banshee fire the laser")

############### B747Fly ################

class B747Fly( Fly):

    def shoot(self):
        print("B747 fire the missile")

############### A380Fly ################

class A380Fly(Fly):

    def shoot(self):
        print("A380 fire the trigeminal shot")
```

```
############## FlyFactory ################

class FlyFactory:

    @staticmethod
    def create(type):
        fly = None
        if (type == 1):
            fly = Banshee()
        elif (type == 2):
            fly = B747Fly()
        elif (type == 3):
            fly = A380Fly()
        return fly


############## test ################

type = int(input("Please select fly 1: Banshee 2: B747 3: A380 \n"))
fly = FlyFactory.create(type)
fly.shoot()
```

Result:

Please select fly 1: Banshee 2: B747 3: A380
2
B747 fire the missile

Builder Pattern Principle

Builder Pattern: Separates object construction from its representation. Separate the construction of a complex object from its representation so that the same construction processes can create different representations.

1. Car divided into three parts: head, body, wheel.

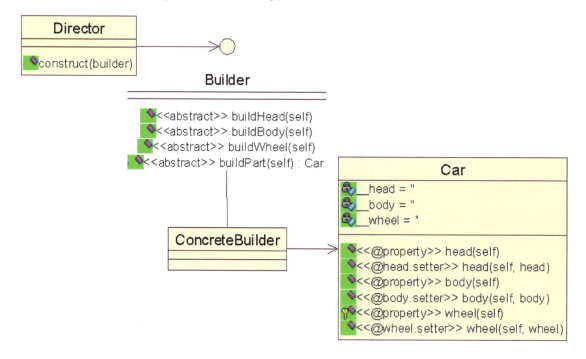

2. Create a Test File : test_builder.py

```python
############### Car #################

class Car:
    __head = ''
    __body = ''
    __wheel = ''

    @property
    def head(self):
        return self.__head

    @head.setter
    def head(self, head):
        self.__head = head

    @property
    def body(self):
        return self.__body

    @body.setter
    def body(self, body):
        self.__body = body

    @property
    def wheel(self):
        return self.__wheel

    @wheel.setter
    def wheel(self, wheel):
        self.__wheel = wheel
```

```python
############### Builder ################

class Builder:

    def buildHead(self):
        pass

    def buildBody(self):
        pass

    def buildWheel(self):
        pass

    def buildPart(self):
        pass

############### ConcreteBuilder ################

class ConcreteBuilder(Builder):
    __car = None

    def __init__(self):
        self.__car = Car()

    def buildHead(self):
        self.__car.head = "Car head construction completed"

    def buildBody(self):
        self.__car.body = "Car body construction completed"

    def buildWheel(self):
        self.__car.wheel = "Car wheel construction completed"

    def buildPart(self):
        return self.__car
```

```
############### Director ################

class Director:

    # Assembled into a car
    @staticmethod
    def construct(builder):
        builder.buildHead()
        builder.buildBody()
        builder.buildWheel()
        return builder.buildPart()

############### test #################

car = Director.construct(ConcreteBuilder())
print(car.head)
print(car.body)
print(car.wheel)
```

Result:

Car head construction completed
Car body construction completed
Car wheel construction completed

Builder Pattern Case

GUI Dialog:

First create prompts, messages and buttons. finally build dialog to pop up.

1. UML Diagram

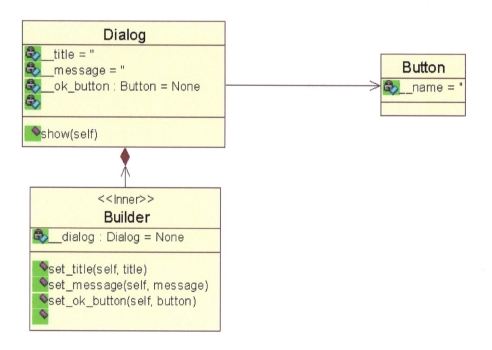

2. Create a Test File : test_dialog.py

```python
############### Button ################

class Button:
    __name = ''

    def __init__(self, name):
        self.__name = name

    @property
    def name(self):
        return self.__name

    @name.setter
    def name(self, name):
        self.__name = name

############### Dialog ################

class Dialog:
    __title = ''
    __message = ''
    __ok_button = None
    __cancel_button = None

    @property
    def title(self):
        return self.__title

    @title.setter
    def title(self, title):
        self.__title = title

    @property
    def message(self):
        return self.__message

    @message.setter
    def message(self, message):
        self.__message = message
```

```python
    @property
    def ok_button (self):
        return self.__ok_button

    @ok_button .setter
    def ok_button (self, ok_button ):
        self.__ok_button = ok_button

    @property
    def cancel_button (self):
        return self.__cancel_button

    @cancel_button .setter
    def cancel_button (self, cancel_button ):
        self.__cancel_button = cancel_button

    def show(self):
        print(self.__title)
        print(self.__message)
        print(self.__cancel_button.name)
        print(self.__ok_button.name)
        print("Popup a dialog")

################ Builder inner class of Dialog ################

    class Builder:
        __dialog = None
        def __init__(self):
            self.__dialog = Dialog()


        def set_title(self, title):
            self.__dialog.title = title

        def set_message(self, message):
            self.__dialog.message = message

        def set_ok_button(self, button):
            self.__dialog.ok_button = button

        def set_cancel_button(self, button):
            self.__dialog.cancel_button = button
```

```
    def create(self):
        return self.__dialog

############### test #################

dialog = Dialog()
builder = dialog.Builder()
builder.set_title("My Dialog")
builder.set_message("message ?")
builder.set_ok_button(Button("Ok"))
builder.set_cancel_button(Button("Cancel"))

dialog = builder.create()
dialog.show()
```

Result:

My Dialog
message ?
Cancel
Ok
Popup a dialog

Adapter Pattern Principle

Adapter Pattern: Match interfaces of different classes.Convert the interface of a class into another interface clients expect. Adapter lets classes work together that couldn't otherwise because of incompatible interfaces.

1. **The original power is 100 voltages, and it needs to be adapted to 36 voltages to work.**

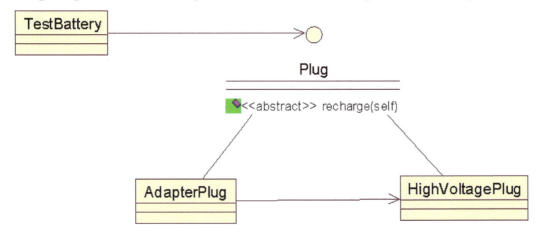

2. Create a Test File : test_battery.py

```python
############### Plug #################

class Plug:

    def recharge(self):
        pass

############### HighVoltagePlug #################

class HighVoltagePlug(Plug):

    def recharge(self):
        return 100 # Power is 100 Voltage
```

```
################ AdapterPlug #################

class AdapterPlug(Plug):

    def recharge(self):
        high_plug = HighVoltagePlug()
        high_voltage = high_plug.recharge()
        low_voltage = high_voltage - 64
        return low_voltage

################ test #################

plug = HighVoltagePlug()
print(plug.recharge(), " too much voltage")

plug = AdapterPlug()
print("Adapter into ", plug.recharge(), " voltage")
```

Result:

```
100  too much voltage
Adapter into  36  voltage
```

Adapter Pattern Case

ListView:

ListView data is filled, the same data but different adapter show different view

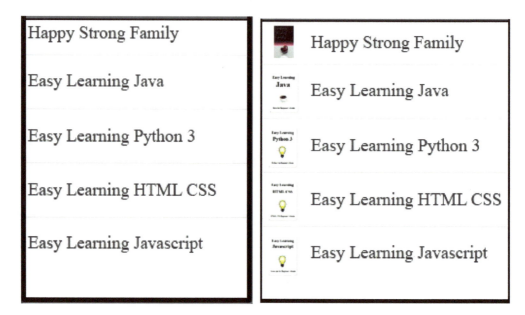

1. UML Diagram

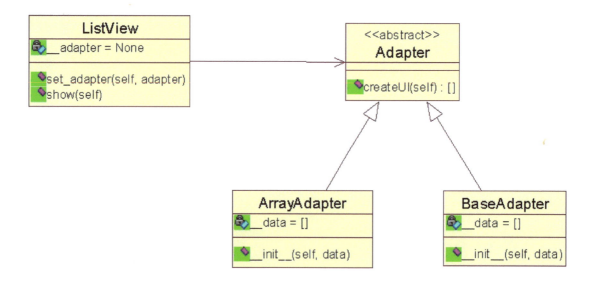

2. Create a Test File : test_adapter.py

```python
############### Adapter ################

class Adapter:

    def createUI(self): # Creating UI display data
        pass

############### ArrayAdapter ################

class ArrayAdapter(Adapter):

    __data = []

    def __init__(self, data):
        self.__data = data

    def createUI(self):
        return self.__data

############### BaseAdapter ################

class BaseAdapter (Adapter):

    __data = []

    def __init__(self, data):
        self.__data = data

    def createUI(self):
        length=len(self.__data)
        for i in range(0,length):
            self.__data[i] = "Image : " + self.__data[i]
        return self.__data
```

```python
############### ListView ################

class ListView:

    __adapter = None

    def set_adapter(self, adapter):
        self.__adapter = adapter

    def show(self):
        data = self.__adapter.createUI()
        for str in data:
            print(str)

############### test ################

data = [
            "Happy Strong Family",
            "Easy Learning Java",
            "Easy Learning Python 3",
            "Easy Learing HTML CSS",
            "Easy Learning Javascript"
        ]

listView = ListView()

listView.set_adapter(ArrayAdapter(data))
listView.show()

print("----------------------------------")

listView.set_adapter(BaseAdapter(data))
listView.show()
```

Result:

Happy Strong Family
Easy Learning Java
Easy Learning Python 3
Easy Learing HTML CSS
Easy Learning Javascript

Image : Happy Strong Family
Image : Easy Learning Java
Image : Easy Learning Python 3
Image : Easy Learing HTML CSS
Image : Easy Learning Javascript

Facade Pattern Principle

Facade Pattern: A single class that represents an entire subsystem. Provide a unified interface to a set of interfaces in a system. Facade defines a higher-level interface that makes the subsystem easier to use.

1. State provide a consistent interface to perform :
Light, music and video.

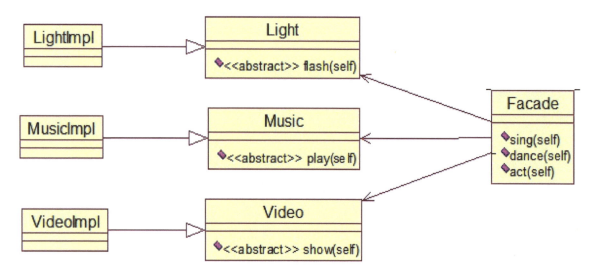

2. Create a Test File : test_facade.py

```
############### Light #################

class Light:

    def flash(self):
        pass

############### LightImpl #################

class LightImpl(Light):

    def flash(self):
        print("Flashing color light")
```

```python
############### Music ################
class Music:

    def play(self):
        pass

############### MusicImpl ################
class MusicImpl(Music):

    def play(self):
        print("Playing classical music")

############### Video ################
class Video:

    def show(self):
        pass

############### VideoImpl ################
class VideoImpl(Video):

    def show(self):
        print("Mountain stream video display")

############### Facade ################

class Facade:

    __light = None
    __music = None
    __video = None

    def __init__(self):
        self.__light = LightImpl()
        self.__music = MusicImpl()
        self.__video = VideoImpl()

    def sing(self):
        print("Start singing with ")
        self.__light.flash()
        self.__music.play()
```

```python
    def dance(self):
        print("Start dancing with ")
        self.__light.flash()
        self.__music.play()
        self.__video.show()

    def act(self):
        print("Start acting with ")
        self.__light.flash()
        self.__video.show()


############### test #################

facade = Facade()

facade.sing();

print("-----------------------------")
facade.dance()

print("-----------------------------")
facade.act()
```

Result:

Start singing with
Flashing color light
Playing classical music

Start dancing with
Flashing color light
Playing classical music
Mountain stream video display

Start acting with
Flashing color light
Mountain stream video display

Facade Pattern Case

1. DBHelper class that provide interface to call the database

If you want to learn MySQL or Oracle please read my book

<<Easy Learning MySQL SQL>>
<<Easy Learning Oracle SQL>>
<<Easy Learning Python 3>>

http://en.verejava.com

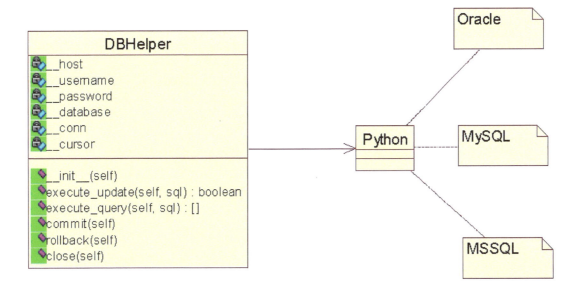

dbhelper.py

```python
import pymysql
import re

class DBHelper:
    __host = "localhost"
    __username = "root"
    __password = "19810109"
    __database = "pythondb"
    __conn = None
    __cursor = None

    # Initialize database connection
    def __init__(self):
        try:
            self.__conn = pymysql.connect(self.__host,self.__username,self.__password,self.__database,charset="utf8")
            self.__cursor = self.__conn.cursor()
        except:
            raise "database connection error"

    # Execute sql statement, return result set
    def execute_query(self,sql):
        try:
            self.__cursor.execute(sql)
            records = self.__cursor.fetchall()
            self.commit()
            return records
        except e:
            print("Sql error : ",e)
            self.rollback()

    # Execute sql statement, add, delete or modify
    def execute_update(self, sql):
        try:
            self.__cursor.execute(sql)
            self.commit()
            return True
        except e:
            print("Sql error : ",e)
            self.rollback()
        return False
```

```python
    # transaction commit
    def commit(self):
        self.__conn.commit()

    # transaction rollback
    def rollback(self):
        self.__conn.rollback()

    # close database connection
    def close(self):
        try:
            if not self.__conn:
                self.__conn.close()
        except e:
            print("database close error : ",e)
```

test_dbhelper.py

```python
from dbhelper import DBHelper

db = DBHelper()

# insert data
sql = "insert into book(title,price)values('Positive thinking',100)"
db.execute_update(sql)

# modify data by id
sql = "update book set price=80 where id=1"
db.execute_update(sql)

# get all book
sql = "select * from book"
results = db.execute_query(sql)
for row in results:
    id = row[0]
    title = row[1]
    price = row[2]
    print ("id=",id,"title=",title," ","price=",price)

db.close()
```

Decorator Pattern Principle

Decorator Pattern: Add responsibilities to objects dynamically. Attach additional responsibilities to an object dynamically. Decorators provide a　　　　flexible alternative to subclassing for extending functionality.

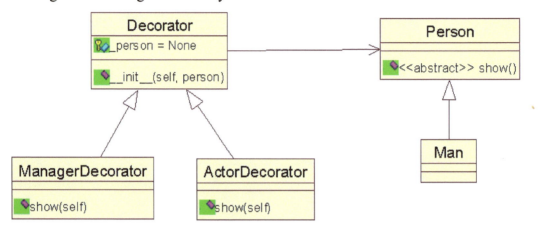

2. Create a Test File : test_decorator.py

```python
############### Person ################

class Person:

    def show(self):
        pass

############### Man ################

class Man(Person):

    def show(self):
        print("I am a man")

############### Decorator ################

class Decorator(Person):

    _person = None

    def __init__(self, person):
        self._person = person
```

44

```python
############### ManagerDecorator ################
class ManagerDecorator(Decorator):

    def __init__(self, person):
        self._person = person

    def show(self):
        self._person.show()
        print("I am still a manager")

############### ActorDecorator ################
class ActorDecorator(Decorator):

    def __init__(self, person):
        self._person = person

    def show(self):
        self._person.show()
        print("I am still an international actor.")

############### test ################
person = Man()
person.show()

print("-----------------------------------")
person = ManagerDecorator(person)
person.show()

print("-----------------------------------")
person = ActorDecorator(person)
person.show()
```

Result:
```
I am a man
-----------------------------------
I am a man
I am still a manager
-----------------------------------
I am a man
I am still a manager
I am still an international actor.
```

Prototype Pattern Shallow Clone

Prototype Pattern : A fully initialized instance to be copied or cloned. Specify the kinds of objects to create using a prototypical instance, and create new objects by copying this prototype.

Shallow clones only copy basic data types

1. Create a Test File : test_shadow_clone.py

```python
import copy

################# Prototype #################

class Prototype:
    __name = ''

    def __init__(self, name):
        self.__name = name

    @property
    def name(self):
        return self.__name

    @name.setter
    def name(self, name):
        self.__name = name
```

```
############### test ################

# Shallow clones only copy basic data types
prototype = Prototype("David")
print("Prototype : ", prototype.name)

prototype_clone = copy.copy(prototype)
print("Prototype Clone : ", prototype_clone.name)

print("-----------------------------")

prototype_clone.name = "Grace"
print("Prototype : ", prototype.name)
print("Prototype Clone : ", prototype_clone.name)
```

Result:

```
Prototype :  David
Prototype Clone :  David
--------------------------------
Prototype :  David
Prototype Clone :  Grace
```

Prototype Pattern Deep Clone

Prototype Pattern : A fully initialized instance to be copied or cloned. Specify the kinds of objects to create using a prototypical instance, and create new objects by copying this prototype.

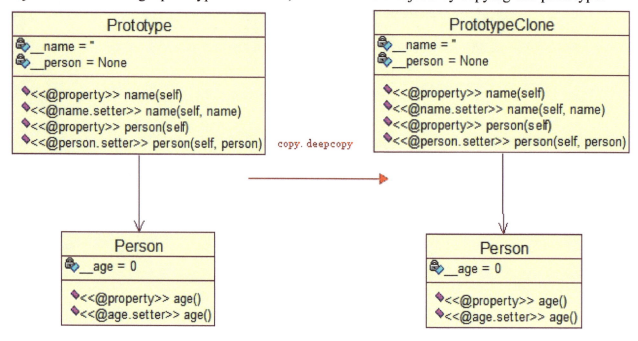

Deep clones can copy object.

1. Create a Test File : test_deep_clone.py

```python
import copy

############### Person #################
class Person:
    __age = 0

    def __init__(self, age):
        self.age = age

    @property
    def age(self):
        return self.__age

    @age.setter
    def age(self, age):
        self.__age = age

############### Prototype #################
class Prototype:
    __name = ''
    __person = None

    def __init__(self, name):
        self.__name = name

    @property
    def name(self):
        return self.__name

    @name.setter
    def name(self, name):
        self.__name = name

    @property
    def person(self):
        return self.__person

    @person.setter
    def person(self, person):
        self.__person = person
```

```
############### test #################

prototype = Prototype("David")
prototype.person = Person(20)
print("Prototype : ", prototype.name, ",", prototype.person.age)

prototype_clone = copy.deepcopy(prototype)
print("Prototype Deep Clone : ",prototype_clone.name, ",", prototype_clone.person.age)

print("-------------------------------------")

prototype_clone.name = "Grace"
prototype_clone.person.age = 30
print("Prototype : ",prototype.name, ",", prototype.person.age)
print("Prototype Deep Clone : ",prototype_clone.name, ",", prototype_clone.person.age)
```

Result:

Prototype : David , 20
Prototype Deep Clone : David , 20

Prototype : David , 20
Prototype Deep Clone : Grace , 30

Bridge Pattern Principle

Bridge Pattern : Separates an object's interface from its implementation. Decouple an abstraction from its implementation so that the two can vary independently.

1. Different people can wear different clothes

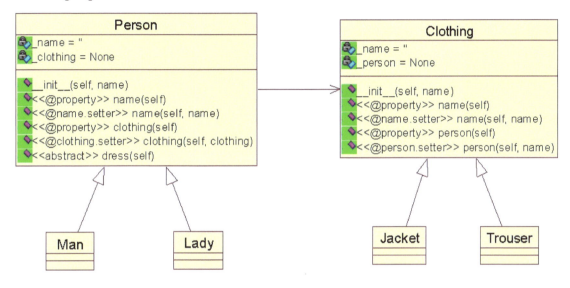

2. Create a Test File : test_bridge.py

```python
############### Person ################

class Person:

    _name = ''
    _clothing = None

    def __init__(self, name):
        self._name = name

    @property
    def name(self):
        return self._name

    @name.setter
    def name(self, name):
        self._name = name

    @property
    def clothing (self):
        return self._clothing

    @clothing .setter
    def clothing (self, clothing ):
        self._clothing  = clothing

    def dress(self):
        pass

############### Man ################

class Man(Person):

    def __init__(self, name):
        self._name = name

    def dress(self):
        print(self._name, " wear " , self._clothing .name)
```

```python
############### Lady ################

class Lady(Person):

    def __init__(self, name):
        self._name = name

    def dress(self):
        print(self._name, " wear ", self._clothing.name)

############### Clothing #################

class Clothing:

    _name = ''
    _person = None

    def __init__(self, name):
        self._name = name

    @property
    def name(self):
        return self._name

    @name.setter
    def name(self, name):
        self._name = name

    @property
    def person(self):
        return self._person

    @person.setter
    def person(self, person):
        self._person = person

############### Jacket ################

class Jacket(Clothing):

    def __init__(self, name):
        self._name = name
```

```python
################ Trouser #################

class Trouser(Clothing):

    def __init__(self, name):
        self._name = name

################ test #################

man = Man("Man")
lady = Lady("Lady")

jacket = Jacket("Jacket")
trouser = Trouser("Trouser")

man.clothing  = jacket # Man wear Jacket
man.dress()

man.clothing  = trouser # Man wear Trouser
man.dress()

lady.clothing  = jacket # Lady wear Jacket
lady.dress()

lady.clothing  = trouser # Lady wear Trouser
lady.dress()
```

Result:

```
Man  wear  Jacket
Man  wear  Trouser
Lady  wear  Jacket
Lady  wear  Trouser
```

Bridge Pattern Case

Bridge Pattern : Separates an object's interface from its implementation. Decouple an abstraction from its implementation so that the two can vary independently.

1. Different airplane fire different bullets

2. UML Diagram

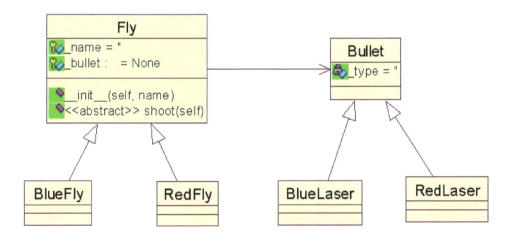

2. Create a Test File : test_fly.py

```python
############### Bullet ################

class Bullet:

    _type = "

    def __init__(self, type):
        self._type = type

    @property
    def type(self):
        return self._type

    @type.setter
    def type(self, type):
        self._type = type

############### BlueLaser ################

class BlueLaser(Bullet):

    def __init__(self, type):
        self._type = type

############### RedLaser ################

class RedLaser (Bullet):

    def __init__(self, type):
        self._type = type
```

```python
############### Fly ##################

class Fly:
    _name = ''
    _bullet = None

    def __init__(self, name):
        self._name = name

    def shoot(self):
        pass

    @property
    def name(self):
        return self._name

    @name.setter
    def name(self, name):
        self._name = name

    @property
    def bullet(self):
        return self._bullet

    @bullet.setter
    def bullet(self, bullet):
        self._bullet = bullet

############### BlueFly ##################

class BlucFly(Fly):

    def __init__(self, name):
        self._name = name

    def shoot(self):
        print(self._name , " fire ",self._bullet.type)
```

```
############### RedFly #################

class RedFly(Fly):
    def __init__(self, name):
        self._name = name

    def shoot(self):
        print(self._name, " fire ", self._bullet.type)

############### test #################

blueFly = BlueFly("BlueFly")
redFly = RedFly("RedFly")

blueLaser = BlueLaser("BlueLaser")
redLaser = RedLaser("RedLaser")

blueFly.bullet = blueLaser # BlueFly fire BlueLaser
blueFly.shoot()

blueFly.bullet = redLaser # BlueFly fire RedLaser
blueFly.shoot()

redFly.bullet = blueLaser # RedFly fire BlueLaser
redFly.shoot()

redFly.bullet = redLaser # RedFly fire RedLaser
redFly.shoot()
```

Result:

```
BlueFly  fire  BlueLaser
BlueFly  fire  RedLaser
RedFly  fire  BlueLaser
RedFly  fire  RedLaser
```

FlyWeight Pattern Case

FlyWeight Pattern : A fine-grained instance used for efficient sharing. Use sharing to support large numbers of fine-grained objects efficiently. A flyweight is a shared object that can be used in multiple contexts simultaneously. The flyweight acts as an independent object in each context — it's indistinguishable from an instance of the object that's not shared.

Some data can be stored in the cache. The client can get the data directly from the cache and improve the query speed.

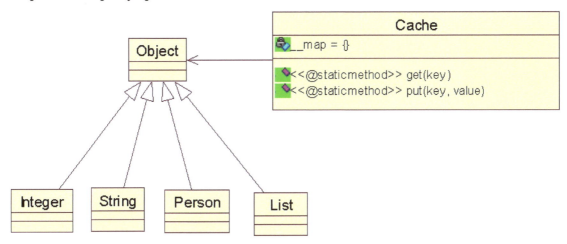

2. Create a Test File : test_cache.py

```python
################# Person #################

class Person:
    __name = ''

    def __init__(self, name):
        self.__name = name

    @property
    def name(self):
        return self.__name

    @name.setter
    def name(self, name):
        self.__name = name
```

```
############### Cache ################

class Cache:
    __map = {}

    @staticmethod
    def get(key):
        return Cache.__map.get(key)

    @staticmethod
    def put(key, value):
        Cache.__map[key] = value

############### test ################

# data are stored in the cache
Cache.put("1", 1000)
Cache.put("name", "Grace")
Cache.put("person", Person("Sala"))

# Get data from the cache
print("int : ", Cache.get("1"))
print("String : ", Cache.get("name"))

person = Cache.get("person")
print("Person Object : ", person.name)
```

Result:

```
int :  1000
String :  Grace
Person Object :  Sala
```

Chain Pattern Principle

Chain Pattern : A way of passing a request between a chain of objects. Avoid coupling the sender of a request to its receiver by giving more than one object a chance to handle the request. Chain the receiving objects and pass the request along the chain until an object handles it.

1. Resignation Apply -> Financial Review -> Manager Review -> Approval

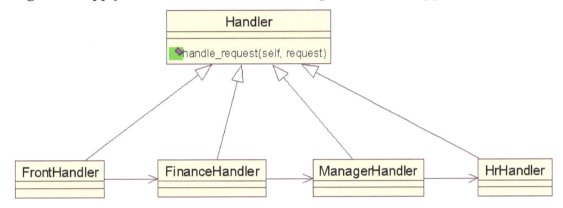

2. Create a Test File : test_handler.py

```
############### Handler ################

class Handler:

    def handle_request(self, request):
        pass

############### FrontHandler ################

class FrontHandler(Handler):
    __nextHandler = None

    def __init__(self, nextHandler):
        self.__nextHandler = nextHandler

    def handle_request(self, request):
        if "ResignationApply" == request:
            print("Resignation Apply")
            if self.__nextHandler != None:
                self.__nextHandler.handle_request("FinancialReview")
```

```python
############### FinanceHandler ################

class FinanceHandler(Handler):
    __nextHandler = None

    def __init__(self, nextHandler):
        self.__nextHandler = nextHandler

    def handle_request(self, request):
        if "FinancialReview" == request:
            print("Financial Review Completed")
            if self.__nextHandler != None:
                self.__nextHandler.handle_request("ManagerReview")

############### ManagerHandler ################

class ManagerHandler (Handler):
    __nextHandler = None

    def __init__(self, nextHandler):
        self.__nextHandler = nextHandler

    def handle_request(self, request):
        if "ManagerReview" == request:
            print("Manager Review Completed")
            if self.__nextHandler != None:
                self.__nextHandler.handle_request("Approval")

############### HrHandler ################

class HrHandler (Handler):
    __nextHandler = None

    def __init__(self, nextHandler):
        self.__nextHandler = nextHandler

    def handle_request(self, request):
        if "Approval" == request:
            print("HR Approval")
            if self.__nextHandler != None:
                self.__nextHandler.handle_request("Approval Completed")
```

```
############### test #################

hr_handler = HrHandler(None)
manager_handler = ManagerHandler(hr_handler)
finance_handler = FinanceHandler(manager_handler)
front_handler = FrontHandler(finance_handler)

front_handler.handle_request("ResignationApply")
```

Result:

Resignation Apply
Financial Review Completed
Manager Review Completed
HR Approval

Chain Pattern Case

Chain Pattern : A way of passing a request between a chain of objects. Avoid coupling the sender of a request to its receiver by giving more than one object a chance to handle the request. Chain the receiving objects and pass the request along the chain until an object handles it.

1. VereWeb Python Web Framework Interceptor

http://en.verejava.com/?section_id=1968727605883

2. Authority Authentication -> Set Character -> Business Preprocessing

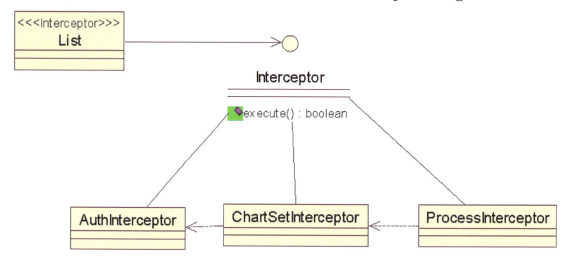

3. Create a Test File : test_intercepter.py

```python
############### Interceptor #################

class Interceptor:

    def execute(self):
        pass

############### AuthInterceptor #################

class AuthInterceptor(Interceptor):

    def execute(self):
        print("Authority Authentication")
        return True
```

```
############### ChartSetInterceptor ################

class ChartSetInterceptor(Interceptor):

    def execute(self):
        print("Set Character")
        return True

############### ProcessInterceptor ################

class ProcessInterceptor(Interceptor):

    def execute(self):
        print("Business Preprocessing")
        return True

############### test ################

interceptor_list = []
interceptor_list.append(AuthInterceptor())
interceptor_list.append(ChartSetInterceptor())
interceptor_list.append(ProcessInterceptor())

for interceptor in interceptor_list:
    is_next_invoke = interceptor.execute()
    if is_next_invoke == False:
        break
```

Result:

Authority Authentication
Set Character
Business Preprocessing

Command Pattern Case

Command Pattern : Encapsulate a command request as an object. Encapsulate a request as an object, thereby letting you parameterize clients with different requests, queue or log requests, and support undoable operations.

1. **Button event, mouse click Ok or Cancel Button.**

2. **UML Diagram**

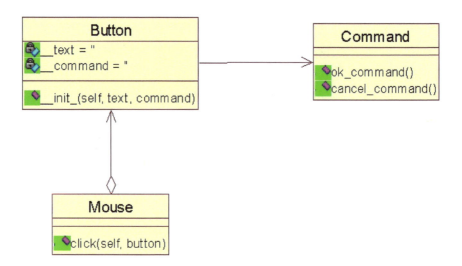

3. Create a Test File : test_command.py

```python
################ Command #################

class Command:

    def ok_command(self):
        print("OK button is clicked")

    def cancel_command(self):
        print("Cancel button is clicked")

################ Button #################

class Button:
    __text = ''
    __command = ''

    def __init__(self, text, command):
        self.__text = text
        self.__command = command

    @property
    def text(self):
        return self.__text

    @text.setter
    def text(self, text):
        self.__text = text

    @property
    def command(self):
        return self.__command

    @command.setter
    def command(self, command):
        self.__command = command
```

```
############### Mouse ################

class Mouse:

    def click(self, command, button):
        getattr(command,button.command)()

############### test #################

command = Command()

button_ok =  Button("Ok", "ok_command")
button_cancel = Button("Cancel", "cancel_command")

mouse = Mouse()
mouse.click(command,button_ok) # Mouse click OK button
mouse.click(command, button_cancel) # Mouse click Cancel button
```

Result:

OK button is clicked
Cancel button is clicked

Iterator Pattern Case

Iterator Pattern : Sequentially access the elements of a collection. Provide a way to access the elements of an aggregate object sequentially without exposing its underlying representation.

1. Implement the iterator in Python

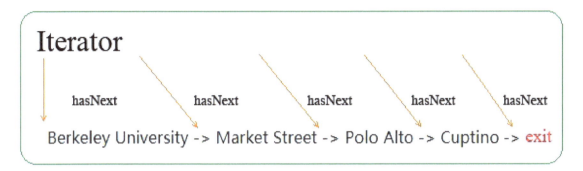

2. UML Diagram

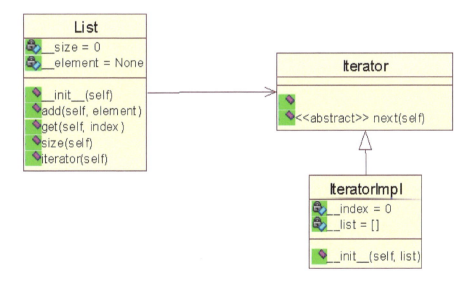

3. Create a Test class : test_iterator.py

```python
############### Iterator ################

class Iterator:

    def has_next(self):
        pass

    def next(self):
        pass

############### IteratorImpl ################

class IteratorImpl(Iterator):
    __index = 0
    __list = None

    def __init__(self, list):
        self.__list = list

    def has_next(self):
        return self.__index < len(self.__list)

    def next(self):
        element = None
        if self.__index < len(self.__list):
            element = self.__list[self.__index]
            self.__index = self.__index + 1
        return element
```

```
############### List ################

class List:
    __size = 0
    __element = None

    def __init__(self):
        self.__element = []

    def add(self, element):
        self.__element.append(element)
        self.__size = self.__size + 1

    def get(self, index):
        return self.__element[index]

    def size(self):
        return size

    def iterator(self):
        return IteratorImpl(self.__element)

############### test ################

list = List()
list.add("Berkeley University")
list.add("Market Street")
list.add("Polo Alto")
list.add("Cuptino")

itcrator = list.iterator()
while iterator.has_next():
    obj = iterator.next()
    print(obj)
```

Result:
Berkeley University
Market Street
Polo Alto
Cuptino

Mediator Pattern Case

Mediator Pattern : Defines simplified communication between classes. Define an object that encapsulates how a set of objects interact. Mediator promotes loose coupling by keeping objects from referring to each other explicitly, and it lets you vary their interaction independently.

1. Client wants to rent a house through an intermediary to contact the HouseOwner

2. UML Diagram

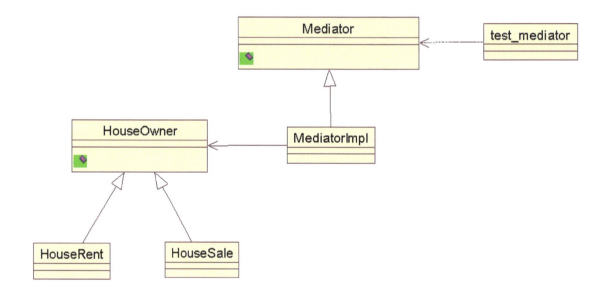

2. Create a Test File : test_mediator.py

```python
############### HouseOwner ################
class HouseOwner:

    def action(self):
        pass

############### HouseRent ################
class HouseRent(HouseOwner):

    def action(self):
        print("Client come to rent a house")

############### HouseSale ################
class HouseSale(HouseOwner):

    def action(self):
        print("Client come to need to sell")

############### Mediator ################
class Mediator:

    def handle(self, content):
        pass

############### MediatorImpl ################

class MediatorImpl( Mediator):
    __owner1 = None
    __owner2 = None

    def __init__(self):
        self.__owner1 = HouseRent()
        self.__owner2 = HouseSale()

    def handle(self, content):
        if content == "rent":
            self.__owner1.action()
        if content == "sale":
            self.__owner2.action()
```

```
############### test #################

mediator = MediatorImpl()

# mediator help adjust the renting and selling between the client and the houseowner
mediator.handle("rent")
mediator.handle("sale")
```

Result:

Client come to rent a house
Client come to need to sell

Memento Pattern Case

Memento Pattern : Capture and restore an object's internal state. Without violating encapsulation, capture and externalize an object's internal state so that the object can be restored to this state later.

1. Notepad++ Undo, redo, history recovery, etc.

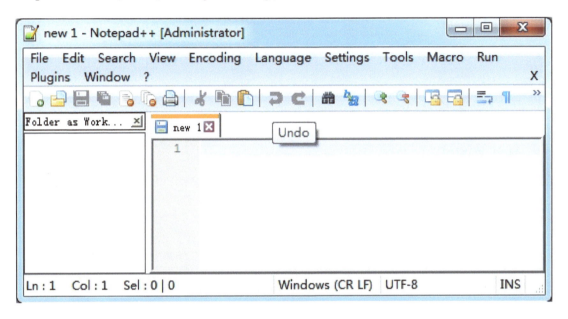

2. UML Diagram

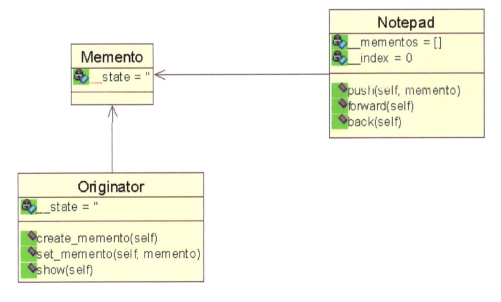

2. Create a Test File : test_memento.py

```python
############### Memonto ################

class Memento:
    __state = ''

    def __init__(self, state):
        self.__state = state

    @property
    def state(self):
        return self.__state

    @state.setter
    def state(self, state):
        self.__state = state

############### Notepad ################

class Notepad:

    __mementos = []
    __index = 0

    def push(self, memento):
        self.__mementos.append(memento)
        self.__index += 1

    def forward(self):
        memento = self.__mementos[self.__index]
        self.__index += 1
        return memento

    def back(self):
        self.__index -= 1
        memento = self.__mementos[self.__index]
        return memento
```

```
############### Originator ################

class Originator:
    __state = ''

    @property
    def state(self):
        return self.__state

    @state.setter
    def state(self, state):
        self.__state = state

    def create_memento(self):
        return Memento(self.__state)

    def set_memento(self, memento):
        self.__state = memento.state

    def show(self):
        print(self.__state)

############### test ################

notepad = Notepad()
# Enter text in Notepad, save while saving
originator = Originator()
originator.state = "Move you in the direction of your dream."
notepad.push(originator.create_memento())

originator.state = "Ways to start your day positively."
notepad.push(originator.create_memento())

originator.state = "Love can change the world."

originator.show()
```

```
# Undo  redo   Recovery history
originator.set_memento(notepad.back())
originator.show()

originator.set_memento(notepad.back())
originator.show()

print("----------------------------")

originator.set_memento(notepad.forward())
originator.show()

originator.set_memento(notepad.forward())
originator.show();
```

Result:

Love can change the world.
Ways to start your day positively.
Move you in the direction of your dream.

Move you in the direction of your dream.
Ways to start your day positively.

Observer Pattern Principle

Observer Pattern : A way of notifying change to a number of classes. Define a one-to-many dependency between objects so that when one object changes state, all its dependents are notified and updated automatically.

1. In the stock market, stock data changes at any time. Sellers and buyers can see changes at any time.

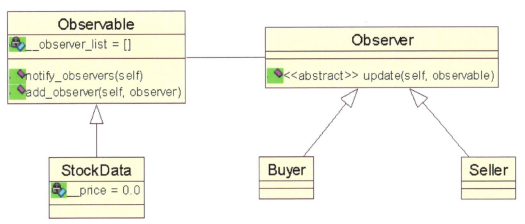

2. Create a Test File : test_observer_observable.py

############### Observable ################

```python
class Observable:

    __observer_list = []

    def notify_observers(self):
        for observer in self.__observer_list:
            observer.update(self)

    def add_observer(self, observer):
        self.__observer_list.append(observer)
```

```python
############### StockData ################

class StockData(Observable):
    __price = 0.0

    def __init__(self, price):
        self.__price = price

    @property
    def price(self):
        return self.__price

    def set_stock_data(self, price):
        self.__price = price
        self.notify_observers()

############### Observer ################

class Observer:

    def update(self, observable):
        pass

############### Buyer ################

class Buyer(Observer):

    def __init__(self, observable):
        observable.add_observer(self)

    def update(self, observable):
        print("Buyer Price :", observable.price)

############### Seller ################

class Seller(Observer):

    def __init__(self, observable):
        observable.add_observer(self)

    def update(self, observable):
        print("Seller Price :", observable.price)
```

```
############### test #################

data = StockData(16.9)

buyer = Buyer(data)
seller = Seller(data)

data.set_stock_data(18.9)

print("-----------------------")

data.set_stock_data(12.9)
```

Result:

```
Buyer Price : 18.9
Seller Price : 18.9
-------------------------
Buyer Price : 12.9
Seller Price : 12.9
```

Visitor Pattern Principle

Visitor Pattern : Defines a new operation to a class without change. Represent an operation to be performed on the elements of an object structure. Visitor lets you define a new operation without changing the classes of the elements on which it operates.

1. A man can successfully
   A woman can successfully
   A man is in love
   A woman is in love

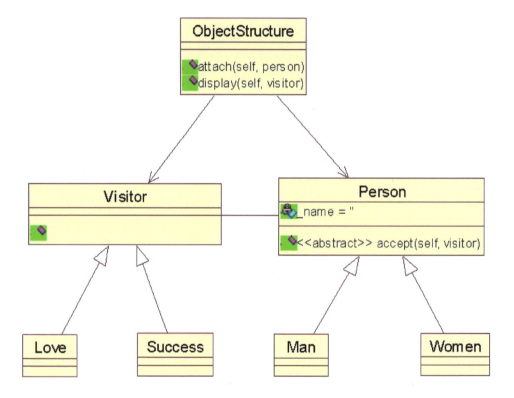

2. Create a Test File : test_visitor.py

```python
############### Person #################
class Person:
    _name = ''

    def accept(self, visitor):
        pass

    @property
    def name(self):
        return self._name

    @name.setter
    def name(self, name):
        self._name = name

############### Man #################
class Man(Person):

    def __init__(self, name):
        self._name = name

    def accept(self, visitor):
        visitor.visit(self)

############### Woman #################

class Woman (Person):

    def __init__(self, name):
        self._name = name

    def accept(self, visitor):
        visitor.visit(self)

############### Visitor #################

class Visitor:

    def visit(self, person):
        pass
```

```python
############### Success #################

class Success(Visitor):

    def visit(self, person):
        print(person.name," successfully")

############### Love #################

class Love (Visitor):

    def visit(self, person):
        print(person.name, " is in love")

############### ObjectStructure #################

class ObjectStructure:
    __persons = []

    def attach(self, person):
        self.__persons.append(person)

    # Traverse various concrete persons and execute their accept methods
    def display(self, visitor):
        for person in self.__persons:
            person.accept(visitor)

############### test #################

object_structure = ObjectStructure()

object_structure.attach(Man("Man"))
object_structure.attach( Woman("Woman"))

object_structure.display(Success())
object_structure.display(Love())
```

Result:
Man successfully
Woman successfully
Man is in love
Woman is in love

State Pattern Case

State Pattern : Alter an object's behavior when its state changes. Allow an object to alter its behavior when its internal state changes. The object will appear to change its class.

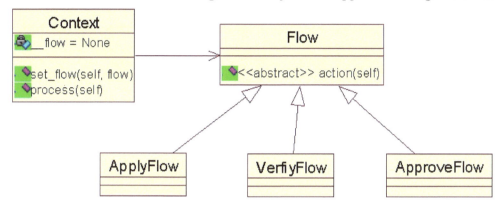

2. Create a Test File : test_state.py

```python
############### Flow #################

class Flow:

    def action(self):
        pass

############### ApplyFlow #################

class ApplyFlow(Flow):

    def action(self):
        print("Apply")

############### VerfiyFlow #################

class VerfiyFlow (Flow):

    def action(self):
        print("Verfiy")
```

```python
############### ApproveFlow ################

class ApproveFlow (Flow):

    def action(self):
        print("Approve")

################ Context #################

class Context:
    __flow = None

    def set_flow(self, flow):
        self.__flow = flow

    def process(self):
        self.__flow.action()

############### test #################

context = Context()
context.set_flow(ApplyFlow())
context.process()

context.set_flow(VerfiyFlow())
context.process()

context.set_flow(ApproveFlow())
context.process()
```

Result:

Apply
Verfiy
Approve

Proxy Pattern Principle

Proxy Pattern : An object representing another object. Provide a surrogate or placeholder for another object to control access to it.

1. Agency registration

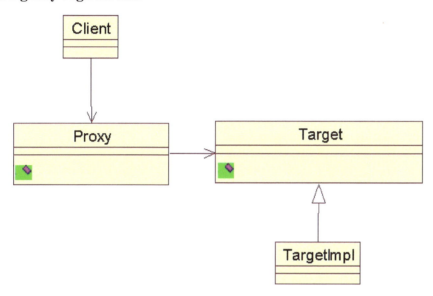

2. Create a Test File : test_proxy.py

```python
############### Target ###################

class Target:

    def do_something(self):
        pass

############### TargetImpl ##################

class TargetImpl(Target):

    def do_something(self):
        print("Agency registration company")
```

```
############## Proxy #################

class Proxy:

    def call(self, target, method):
        print("before")
        result = getattr(target, method)()
        print("after")
        return result

############### test #################

target = TargetImpl()
proxy = Proxy()
proxy.call(target, "do_something")
```

Result:

before
Agency registration company
after

Thanks for learning, please study book
https://www.amazon.com/dp/B08C9619XH

If you enjoyed this book and found some benefit in reading this, I'd like to hear from you and hope that you could take some time to post a review on Amazon. Your feedback and support will help us to greatly improve in future and make this book even better.

You can follow this link now.

http://www.amazon.com/review/create-review?&asin=1098531027

Different country reviews only need to modify the amazon domain name in the link:
www.amazon.co.uk
www.amazon.de
www.amazon.fr
www.amazon.es
www.amazon.it
www.amazon.ca
www.amazon.nl
www.amazon.in
www.amazon.co.jp
www.amazon.com.br
www.amazon.com.mx
www.amazon.com.au

I wish you all the best in your future success!

www.ingramcontent.com/pod-product-compliance
Lightning Source LLC
Chambersburg PA
CBHW041427050326
40689CB00003B/690